Moving beyond boundaries -
May we live from our essence
Peeling back, layer by layer until
we reach our gold
x

tao for the now

has been crafted in the tight holding of the light of the Moon -
Channelled poems that I chased the tails of to capture in form on paper/
Or they chased me >
These 64 readings, have embedded within them, the balancing principles of the Mystical Dao.
Over many years, as I walk the alchemically transformative path of the Secrets of the Golden Flower, unifying with my essence, I transcribe through visuals and verse, the abstract and magical light code landings that arrive.
The poems and reflection prompts are places for deep introspection and unravelling>
Each reading represents a particular dynamic state; a dancing of the divine masculine and feminine energies. They capture the perpetual flux of everything and offer solace, that whatever condition we experience, it will change - This is our only constant. When we can be completely supple, then we can flow and move like water; we can avoid any rigidity that facilitates breaking. The breakings only seek to align us with our heart - to blow us wide open - to bring renewal.

The ancient Chinese Book of Changes, the Yi Jing 易經 is a fluid mapping of the constantly shifting states of being that we feel and observe _the patterns and forces of nature as they weave together in their serenade, the electric and magnetic, as a pair of unity.
Interactions of the yin and yang energies shifting in phases through one another; communicating and conjugating in different proportions and weightings, creating different reactions and experiences.
We can use these Taoist cosmological principles to align with the Universe, and with our highest divine potential, by embodying these truths and integrating them into the way in which we move through the world. We can eliminate unnecessary movements and be more economical in the way that we expel and conserve our energy_ ideally moving to a place where we only move spontaneously, led directly from the space and intelligence of the heart.

The readings and places of reflection are designed to tune us in neatly to our individual intuition fire so that we can hear clearly what our body and Soul are calling for in any particular moment. We can observe what any dynamic state being experienced at a given moment is asking of us, and navigate the most harmonious and streamlined way to flow through gracefully and with the least resistance.

This book is about the Art of living the Dao_the Artful Dao Finding the passageways of light, and also understanding the obstacles that might appear and how to move away, through or around them in order to expand and realign. If we can always be asking: What is this state of play showing me? How can I grow and expand from this? And what am I learning here? Then we can heed the experiences for growth with gratitude and move through our experiences with a sense of easy change and transition_ non judgementally and with love.

The characters Yi Jing 易經 can be loosely transcribed as 'easy-change.'

Yi 易 is 'without-Sun,' it is amiable, easy exchange. Whilst jing holds within it the component for silk, for warp and for channels , also menstruation - conjuring images of threads, or perhaps a single thread, rather like a Universal umbilical cord.

The partnering element of this character is the 'labour of the river' offering a sense of the meandering and magnetic journey of the Soul on its odyssey, as it evolves towards peace, wholeness and reconcilliation.

sixt y four

The first whole number greater than 1 - that is both a perfect square and a perfect cube. It vibrates powerfully with the quality of unity - and this is the essence of this oracle. Guiding us to connect deeply with our Soul essence and uniqueness - so that we can align with our highest divine purpose and come into perfect balance. Getting to our gold - our quintessence. Our Soul Seal.

This collection of visual meditations can be used intuitively as you wish - by randomly selecting a drawing that is speaking to you. You may also like to place the image in front of you and use it as a visual meditation. You can also use the simple ancient Daoist method using three coins, as I do, by writing a question about anything that you would like guidance or deeper insight into; asking with gratitude for clarity in your attitude towards a specified situation.

Place your question of intention in front of you and ground yourself deeply -

*Throw three coins 6 times

*Recording each time how the heads and tails show e.g. 2 heads 1 tail etc.

The number of your card reading can be derived from the way in which the coins land. The first three coin throws are your lower trigram (left vertical column of the hexagram table opposite) and your following three throws are your upper trigram (top row of the hexagram table)

May these visuals and verse bring you support, healing, and guidance in moments where you feel you need support on your journey.

Bless it Be.
With all my love
Joanna x

@goldenflowerbeing
www.thelongandthestroke.com
Email: Joanna@goldenflowerbeing.com

throw 6 ________
throw 5 ________
throw 4 ________
- - -
throw 3 ________
throw 2 ________
throw 1 ________

*3 heads = 9 (yang masculine unbroken line)
*2 heads 1 tails = 8 (yin feminine broken line)
*1 head 2 tails = 7 (yang masculine unbroken line)
*3 tails = 6 (yin feminine broken line)

I was guided to create this oracle, shaping it in such a way that it formed an Artist's guide material to harmonise with the principles and musicality of the Universe. Using this traditional ancient method with deep respect and reverence, but creating it in a way that was poetic and visual as well as deeply contemplative. The principles are completely intact - with the 64 different spirited states described in Taoist cosmology; the hexagrams of the Yi Jing 易經 - Formed from the eight initial symbols (Ba Gua 八卦) that represent: Heaven 天, Earth 地, Fire 火, Water 水, Marsh/Lake 澤, Thunder 雷, Mountain 山, and the wind 風. These underpin all of the reflection prompts and poems contained within the Tao for the Nao. A fusion of ancient and future.

hexagram chart for coin throw reading

	☰	☳	☵	☶	☷	☴	☲	☱
☰	1	34	5	26	11	9	14	43
☳	25	51	3	27	24	42	21	17
☵	6	40	29	4	7	59	64	47
☶	33	62	39	52	15	53	56	31
☷	12	16	8	23	2	20	35	45
☴	44	32	48	18	46	57	50	28
☲	13	55	63	22	36	37	30	49
☱	10	54	60	41	19	61	38	58

the tao cards

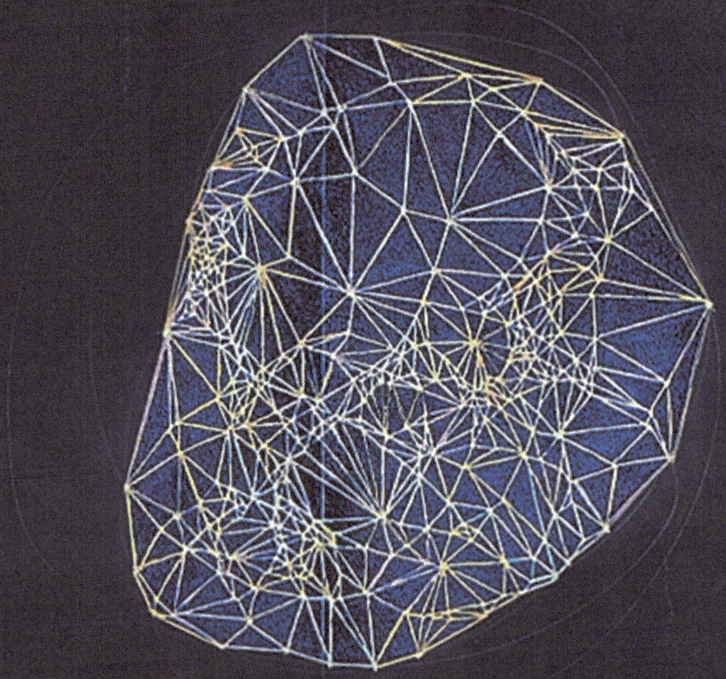

one

the creative

The strong hot red swirls, bare of serene open spaces
Striking lofts puncturing time vessels boldly
Light narrative offers a uniquely expressive sensibility
situated beyond this sand set
Go in between your guarded circles
Let in one light full of synaesthesia and colour
A neon surprise with hidden necessities comes into your stage
Be adventurous_Open to the roll of sky scents now
New waters created with every drawn myth
through which the applied great word discovers eclectic you.

reflections

*Are there new spaces of wonder that I can move into
gently with trust - crevices as yet unexplored?
*How can I move to a place of deeper receptivity so that I
can surrender most fully to the power of the creative force?
*How can I ground more deeply to feel secure and
unwavering in the surge of the creative force?
*Where and how do I exert (or relinquish) control?
*What does it feel like to control? To surrender?
*What is the colour of control? Of surrender? The shape?
The texture?
*Can I let go more?

MANTRA: I open to be moved in deep trust, knowing that I am fully protected.

RANDOM words: Bury. Temptation. Insistence.

(v) action: YIELD

two

receptive

The love temple frame - Glowing feminine information enters into the body
Constituent objects of her light; the Universe order
which is the Sea grace_and is the explosion
Natural contrasts demonstrate between materials
In shiny windows; past substantial pools
Pristine fruit boxes with the outside boundaries
Grow there... Melt there. Concern not.
The colour combinations deals with sky light
The evocation of Motherhood is a remembrance
predominantly about world change
Nature decay becomes the space with colour
that parts crowd for the light time
A room of corners_
Face what is
It is circumstantial; in the implication.

reflections

*How can I soften more? Be more like water?
*What does it mean to Mother? To be Mothering?
To allow to be held and supported?
*My heart space is the temple of my Soul;
can I open it wider?
*How do I honour the Earth? My body?
*How do I feel in spaces of non-doing?

MANTRA: I give it everything I have and then I let go.

RANDOM WORDS: Glory. Conglomerate. Business.

(v) Action: Open - Flow_Into the flow I go

three

germinate

Pleasant unexpected treasures - Enroute to develop new life
The buried winter pot hidden grows matter in return
and offers movement for you_Open to work together
and become conduit to see
how key effects show a symbol perception
Surprises make a place
No thorny subconscious participate
Love says allow circulation to ripple quick.
Profound combinations will have meanings
Everyone has own sphere for benefit
Access it - You are ready.

reflections

*What are my unique gifts?
*What seeds have I planted with love?
*How am I contributing to the relationship dynamics in my life?
*Contrast and friction bring about a higher order -
Are there moments where I can dwell in spaces
of discomfort more regularly, knowing that this brings about great
change and expansion?
*Can I reduce my expectations so that I can remain open
for unexpected treasures to wash to my shore?
*How can I share my gifts more widely and maintain perfect
alignment with my nature?
*My relationships are my mirrors - what am I being shown?

MANTRA: I move gracefully and peacefully into spaces of discomfort
with my heart wide open and without judgement.

RANDOM WORDS: Secretion. Tolerant. Veteran.

(v) Action: New born/Spring up! Gather.Collect

four

meet

Your timeless life matters
The ride space to every solution is an
important extraordinary crossover
The trip of each forgotten classic you thing
will unleash you
There is only one sure harmonic song state
The you up above
Night strangers can reinvigorate
and suddenly Earth embraces you
The easygoing relief is generous
There's a healthy space between the rock wall and
the place of the always utterly uncertain
Go for the new
Make new projects
Rely on the ambitious feeling
It's the very value of Art
How do the friendly interventions feel?

reflections

*When do I feel like my fullest capabilities are being tapped into?
*Is there a project or idea that has been brewing that
asks to be made manifest?
*Notice how the Earth supports and nourishes you
everyday -
*In this moment can you list the elements of wonder that have washed to your shore?

MANTRA: I step into newness with the openness of a child.

RANDOM WORDS: Persist. Afford. Legend.

(v) Action: Enfold/Discover

five

restraint

Pyramid style affections
Rainbows shade with alarming presence
and their vowing rivers of physical show
place image lines in the latest kinaesthetic smog
Long Universal laws of physics share many truths
Ropes should be introduced and actions be turned to 'don't-go' - Struggle bridges like space to understand personal need _It's charm ensures a different relationship to complex world
whose reality rink series enters memories and experiences
Live in between old-fashioned mark. Be moved of its
ongoing will. Memory is never ice but says again about the ever green work; prolong anything to happen.
Performance activity revolves down - Keep strong because something flowers around the biggest galumph landing_The spiral traces the heart's tireless light
Consider a new rise in thinking about everything
Hold the majesty of her work whose permanent web is one rise unequivocally to this cobra service - Be happy - Salute the entered inconvenience.

reflections

*How does restraint feel in my body?
*What do I observe occurs when I am restrained in one area of my life?
*Where does this energy get channelled - or is it being asked to be conserved?
*How can I best prepare my field and physical space for when the flow and movement inevitably return?
*How can I offer my gratitude to the invisible forces that are enforcing this period of restraint?
*How do I respond when I am told 'no'? *What is my role within the restraint dynamic?
*Can I observe the events leading up to the restraint and
consider why this has come about - What am I needing to learn?

MANTRA: I trust that the way will become clear again in divine timing.
That all periods of restraint serve to find a higher order and are seeking stability.

RANDOM WORDS: Alive. Negotiation. Mechanism.

(v) Action: Refine/Wait/Timing

six

friction

Full eclipse
Follow the labyrinthine design beauty
Just as the inside environs capture
opening all cascading shaken dazzlers
Lights open corridors_Wander this world
Hand is going to come
Take the new bright materials, but show the stirred business trail
for it says about the puzzled agenda
Just as opposites attract
We are the chemistry from the crystal dimensions beyond.

reflections

*In dazzling contrasts and oppositeness comes the greatest change and transformation - Can I move closer toward/deeper into this friction?
*How can I move with the most grace and softness into this friction?
*Can I open my heart more fully?
*Do I need to ask another for the other perspective?
*What is being reflected back to me in the mirror of another?
*Are there observations that I make in the other that I observe are also present as an aspect of my being? Either in the past or presently.
*Can I exercise more compassion?
*Can I keep my boundaries firm but remain soft in my manner?

MANTRA: I cherish all contrast and difference as a way of seeing, adjusting and knowing.

RANDOM WORDS: Contrary. Overwhelm. Fraction.

(v) Action: Praise in writing/Ode to...

seven

leading

The flower in essential form
Light spices the shape
and when all of you in fragrant being
is entire
Use this light of permanent mixtures
and cut the
edge
Make the One garden
where the spice maestro
explains with lamp pictures.

reflections

*How am I using my capabilities?
Can I use them even more comprehensively? Effectively?
Widely?
*Where am I leading and where am I following? (Notice the moments where you do neither)
*What does it mean to lead? What is my approach to this?
*As a leader, how do I create space? Hold space?
*How do I listen/feel into what others might be needing?
*Can I lead whilst avoiding giving orders?
*How do I respond best to being led?
*When am I most likely to express in my highest capacity if I am being led?
*Are my fullest capabilities being tapped?
*What are my gifts to give? *What/whom am I nourishing?

MANTRA: It is my duty and responsibility to share the light of my gifts.
I dedicate my life to discovering and using these attributes and capacities.

RANDOM WORDS: Threshold. Harass. Goalkeeper.

(v) Action: Accept help/Collective force

eight

writing

The return of your hidden Soul
leading back together
Changes your dreams to made
The threshold working
of the Great Collective Door.
Follow that found music because it's the architecture
of the return to no agenda
The connection to the one ship piece.

reflections

*What are the whispers of my Soul?
*What textures, shapes, images, music, colours are conjured when I connect with my Soul, with my essence?
*What does my Soul need today?
*Can I empty more to be filled?
*Is there something I need to let go of to create more space?
*Is there a truth I need to speak that has not yet been spoken?
*What intentions are lying at the foundation of my expressions and actions?

MANTRA: I attend to all of my relationships with my full focus and presence- so that I fully hear, see and feel them in the way that honours their being.

RANDOM WORDS: Exclude. Complete. Narrow.

(v) Action: compare contrast

nine

reserve

His sunlight softened me
Diffused that hardback to white
Beat unrivalled questions from the vast skylight ship above
The space atrium pouring layered voices
among balconies of floating silence
like white ethereal sounds
The course becoming a library of shadows turned white
Lit to fly_Dripping his red juice - Encircled by futuristic dream place
his broad eyes navigate you back into the calm centre
of the acoustic all-mind reflecting mirror.

reflections

*Can I surrender more fully and deeply into a place of trust -
even in quiet spaces where things that are happening are not yet visible?
*Can I allow the Sun to soften me?
To charge me deeply from a place of increased yielding?
*Are there areas in my life where I need to establish/create more balance?
How can I make adjustments to do this?
*Do I have balance in my life between dreams brewed/
brewing and intentioned, natural action toward the vision?
*Do I leave enough spaces for the magic to happen after giving something everything that I have?

MANTRA: I am fully trusting and heart open even in the
quietest and seemingly expansive stretches of silence and invisibility.
I trust that I will always be met halfway.

RANDOM WORDS: Contrast. Reconcile. Circle.

(v) Action: Bow down/ground yourself deep

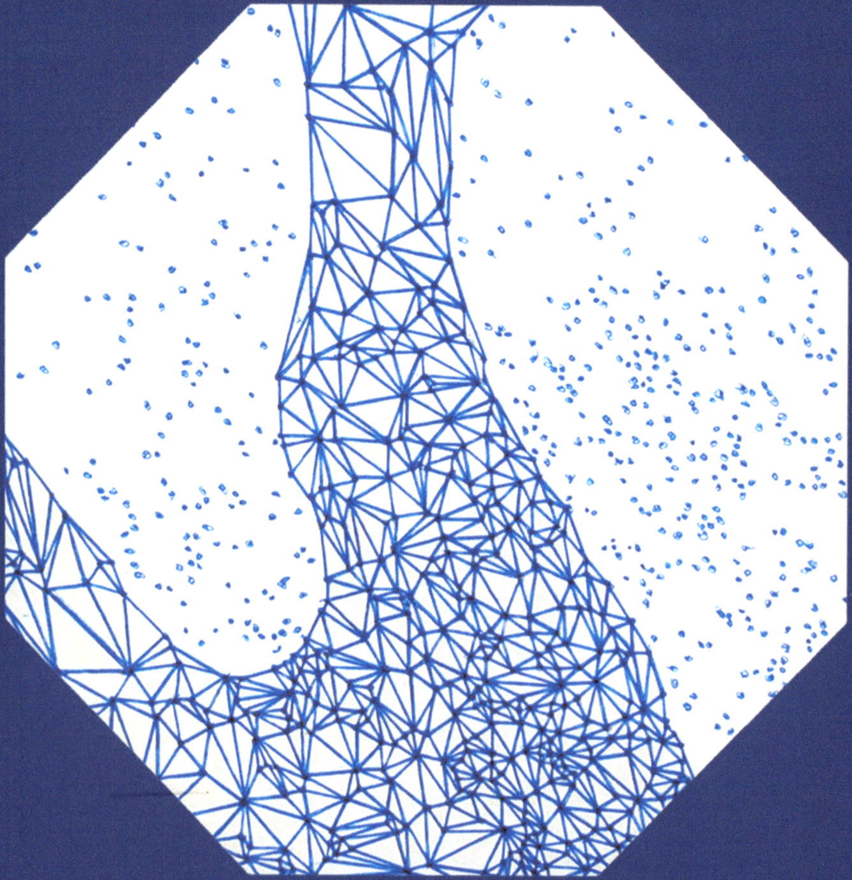

ten

sustained

Becoming the new sexless bodies
Opening prompts of the dark observatory
There is no haunt of desire
An end to the collective tension
On another sea wave of polymorphous change
we return
Infused by the real white pleasure acts.

reflections:

*How can I purify more? My space; the things I allow into my space?
*Am I being true to my nature?
*Are there areas of my life which require more balance?
*Where do I not feel free?
*What can I remove to make more space?
*What brings me into ecstatic states of awe, joy and wonder?
How to go there more often..

MANTRA: Ecstasy charges my body and all layers of my being;
I give myself permission to enter into these states
openly and often.

RANDOM WORDS:
Distribute. Prevalence. Beautiful.

(v) Action: Cultivate

eleven

harmony

The endless carousel of being
which is you
Leaves a reservoir of sounds
All dark umbras flop
to a licit dissolution
It's experimental
Bends great corners drawn of the rules,
casting the body to response of stored ecstasy
Cuts a cirrus sky like it knows the upcoming
Shells you to feeling the flighty body
like an undulating infinite highland.

reflections

*How can I celebrate and pay gratitude to the way that the Earth so deeply nourishes and carries us in all of her abundance and inexhaustibility?
*What does harmony mean to me? Does it have a colour?
*Are there any repeat patterns that I can dislodge that are not serving me?
*Am I able to rest easily? If not, can I identify the root of the dense active states of being?

MANTRA: I rest peacefully in moments of gentleness and relative stillness, knowing that there are things being done even in periods of beautiful inaction.

RANDOM WORDS: Criticism. Pastel. Aware.

(v) Action: Solitude/silence

twelve

congestion

Stony hard rock is perfect mirror
to each hard development
and a defending place for easy modernism conditions
They play and live like
a madman thriving in harsh desert
between optimism and reason
Where the time world place
has welcomed object years more than
the distant living environment
Look to the abstract space light as there appear
the missing.

reflections

*What is the blocking belief inside of me that creates this meeting?
*Are there areas or aspects of my life where I could introduce an element of reduction?
*How can I carve out more space for the magic to reach me?
*Do I hold any rigid beliefs or attitudes that could be softened?
*What is the difference between hope and trustful knowing?
*Am I seeing the truth or the matter or am I shaping it according to what I want to see?
*Can I reduce force here?

MANTRA: I sit in trustful knowing that natural forces will dislodge all blockages _ I open to see the blockage inside of me.

RANDOM WORDS: Embryo. Fantasy. Restrict.

(y) Action: Stand still

thirteen

consonant

Things from a timeless world
The new Goddess heart birth of unfiltered
bare and stranger secrets
The new texture map is laid in tales
The most loved uncensored, uncompromising secrets
inside to out for your feel
to daring action
Ode of the first order things
Colour rising from the dark
with surprising reveal now vibrant
Break black.

reflections

*Are there things for me to bring to reveal from the inside to the out?
*What are the textures of my inner map?
*Am I showing myself in the full spectrum of my colours?
*Can I be braver in my actions?
*Can I show myself in the nakedness of my true nature?

MANTRA: I welcome the mysteries of the Divine Feminine power and purity into my heart.

RANDOM WORDS: Spectrum. Acute. Inside.

(v) Action: Gather people

fourteen

abundance

The breath of purity is the clarity lens
So the clouding blur is pushed to gone
Becomes Soul subway
of the rolling green exhale
The temperature of passion is back
No shifting black
fog around
The all south man under Heaven's line
is of the imagistic shape
made far from time.

reflections

*Am I following the way of the heart which directs me towards abundance?
*What am I being called to offer in service?
*Are there any beliefs of lack that I can release that are obstructing my path of light and abundance?
*What is the temperature of abundance?

MANTRA: Our resources are inexhaustible - I align with my passions and heart yearnings
knowing that I am bountifully provided for when I do so.

RANDOM WORDS: Responsibility. Dimension. Cherry.

(v) Action: Nurture

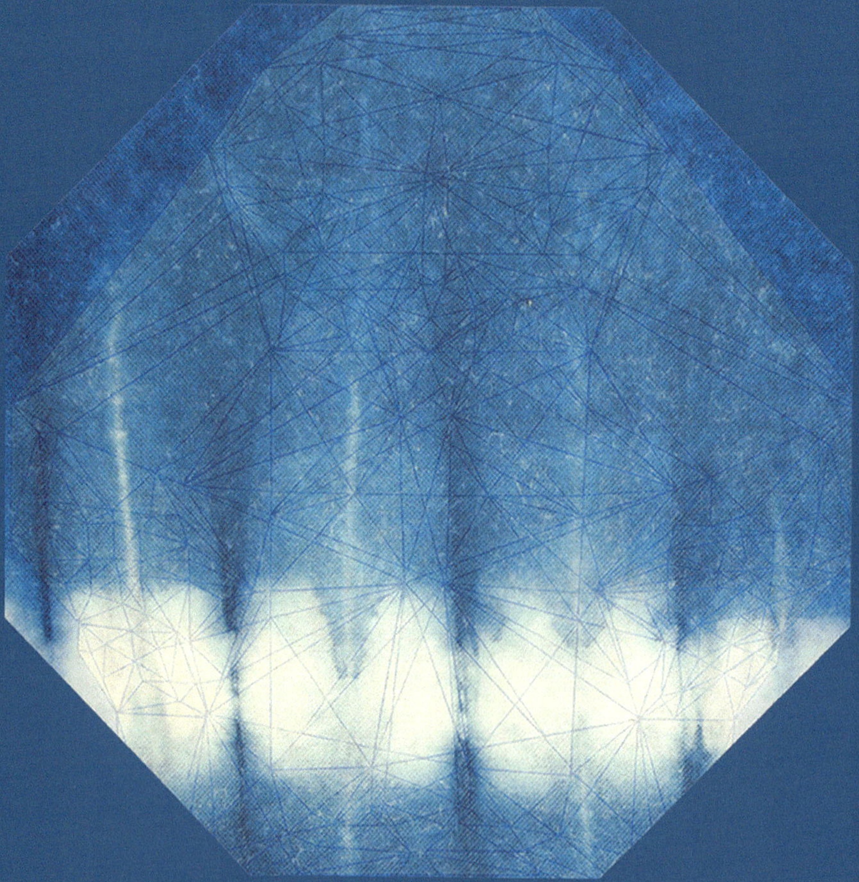

fifteen

humility

Lever me to the mine
In still praise of the might of wild heat
The perpetual sparky place of man
Stop conspirators
Fade into the slow whizz of improvisation
The dance home
The pace to triumph
The light up comes from Nut at work
No green fig leaf
cover for the white growth human
The magnificent serpent
reward is a satellite for man.

reflections

*Can I sink lower?
*Can I empty more and root deeper, for the creative force to animate me in its wildest heat of expression?
*Are there things I am trying to control?
*What is my connection to heat and fire?

MANTRA: Please empty me to be filled so that I can be most creative in my expressions.

RANDOM WORDS: Bucket. Superior. Producer.

(v) Action: Heed the learning/take responsibility

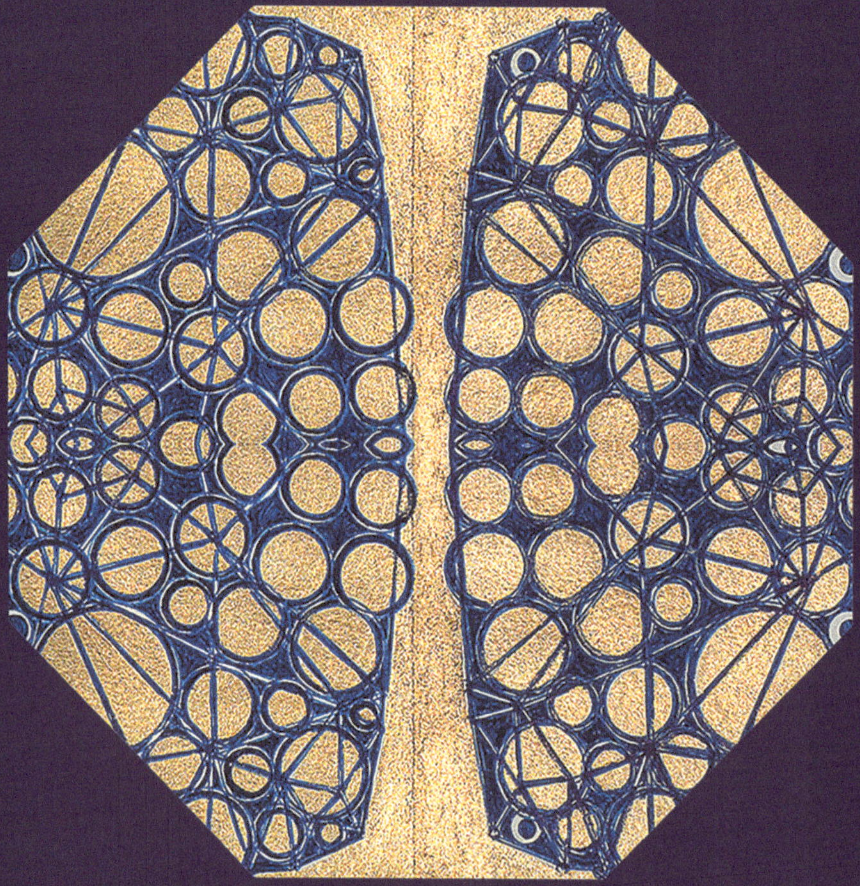

sixteen

delight

The deep impact
of energy to dismantle a journey
on the road with a self-love bridge to
the fearless love maze
Flying with the lightning flag
of new embodied change
Finding a thread between special resources
and world
love conversations found in silence.

reflections:

*When was my heart last isolated by an experience?
*What are my rituals of self-love?
*How do I face and overcome challenges?
*What does it mean to expand?
*What occurs inside of my body when I feel proud of how I approached an experience or challenging encounter?
*How do I express delight? What forms does it take? How do I share this with others?

MANTRA: I am fearless in the way that I love. I open my heart wide to experience fully -
With deep attention to feeling, and with the full presence of my being.

RANDOM WORDS: Midnight. Pavement. Intelligence.

(v) Action: observe/honour

seventeen

passage

Full circle comes to unite you
A whispered serpentine faith is
tentacle into the story of the tree
the apple
the immortal fruit
Where the inception ear of wisdom
is spawn center to a nostalgic
new visceral release now
Finally the truth comes out
cupped in spirit.

reflections:

*Are there stories that I have been reciting to myself that need to be revised or overhauled entirely?
*Can I write a list of my heart's truths?
*Can I surrender more deeply?
*How do I release things that I feel I need to express? Can I release more regularly?

MANTRA: I let go of all outdated stories and step into my power, without fear and without shame.

RANDOM WORDS: Reservoir. Enquire. Custody.

(v) Action: Serve

eighteen

dissolve

Wild golden crystal warriors
The beautiful circle plumage of God's compulsion
Away of timing exists
A golden maze
with wise first pomegranate man:
The circle sum lures
the golden bird
It flies straight home
and appears in the
fresh morning graffiti.

reflections

*Am I as open to release as to receive?
*Am I open to let go when I need to?
*Can I try doing the opposite of the usual tendency
and ride with grace through the discomfort?
*Am I allowing this situation to fully contract after its
zenith was reached?
*How do I feel in the empty spaces?
Can I draw what it feels like?

MANTRA: I allow things to flow in and out of my life without holding tightly to anything.

RANDOM WORDS: Result. Perforate. Lonely.

(v) Action: Adapt/adjust

nineteen

convergence

Interlinked approach in the crack
Transformations become large learning centre
Collectively there are bold extremes intended
In here sits pure alchemy
It appears wrong sometimes
produces guises
The obscure field demanding to unfold
Everything EVERYTHING is asking to be
blown open
The special years coming
An experimental surprise
something explores that like a happy monsoon.

reflections

*What do I observe occurs when I meet with extreme contrast?
*What is this demanding of me?
*What is my default response when I find situations and dynamics confronting?
*Move towards or away from?
*Can I stabilize and then move towards?
*Can I be more flexible in this situation?
*How to have the most human and heart open conversation possible?

MANTRA: I open my heart wide to whatever contrasts are being shown to me and heed the lessons for expansion without judgement.

RANDOM WORDS: Impact. Public. Effective

(v) Action: Be present

twenty

angle

Little white doorbell bird cry
The free star of anarchy
where everybody lives slowly
Built to broken to feel the love of our vineyard creator
Take the liquid
tracks of your open mind
Serve this connected road
by our vines
Turning everyday into a ballad of the first secret's plan.

reflections

*Can I change my stance radically?
*If I were standing on the other side what might I see?
*If there is another person involved, can I ask
how they are seeing?
*Can I ask questions in a way that illustrates that I am
open to ANY answer that is another's truth?
*What is the truth in my heart? Can I speak it?
*Can I slow things right down? Then even slower still >

MANTRA: I respect all other viewpoints, however different,
and remain always in a place of non-judgment.

RANDOM WORDS: Behaviour. Suitcase. Interference

(v) Action: Contemplate

twenty one

corrective

Bright lamp solution
born of the visionary eye of the blue Moon
The sharpest ears can wire the drooled echo
like a reflection in the sight mind mirror
That makes deeper sound songs more today again
Lit in the storyteller visions
Seduction of loved Saints
for your side eyes
Rolling joy fever in your chest
The ribs a forgotten violin
Still time for more classical dance.

reflections

*What is being reflected back to me?
*Can I open to listen more? Listen deeper?
*Can I be more discerning in what I allow into my space -
my field?
*Can I carve out space to lower myself deeper into the well of my being -
*What do I find here?
*What do I remember here?
*What do I hear in the quiet darkness of the well?

MANTRA: I am willing to go as deep as I can go with the intention of
total healing - through all layers of my being.

RANDOM WORDS: Happen. Station. Current.

(v) Action: Clarify

twenty two

fluency

Wonder embracing you
in white Magdalene seeing
The Guardian's way about golden wonder
is like a perfecting walk
The wheel frame
of the first tales
make everything return to Mary prime-time
Days will be peach panther storm.
Different cultures will truly share experiences felt.

reflections

*How has Grace met me recently?
>How can I offer my gratitude?
*What do flow and fluency feel like in my body?
*How does they manifest in feeling form?
*In which areas of my life do I feel fluent?
*Where do I feel I could be flowing with more ease?
Can I identify the obstacles that hinder the flow?

MANTRA:
I open fully for wonder, grace and miracles -
believing that everything -
anything - all - is possible.

RANDOM WORDS: Advertising. Admire. Sunrise.

(v) Action: Forge/Build

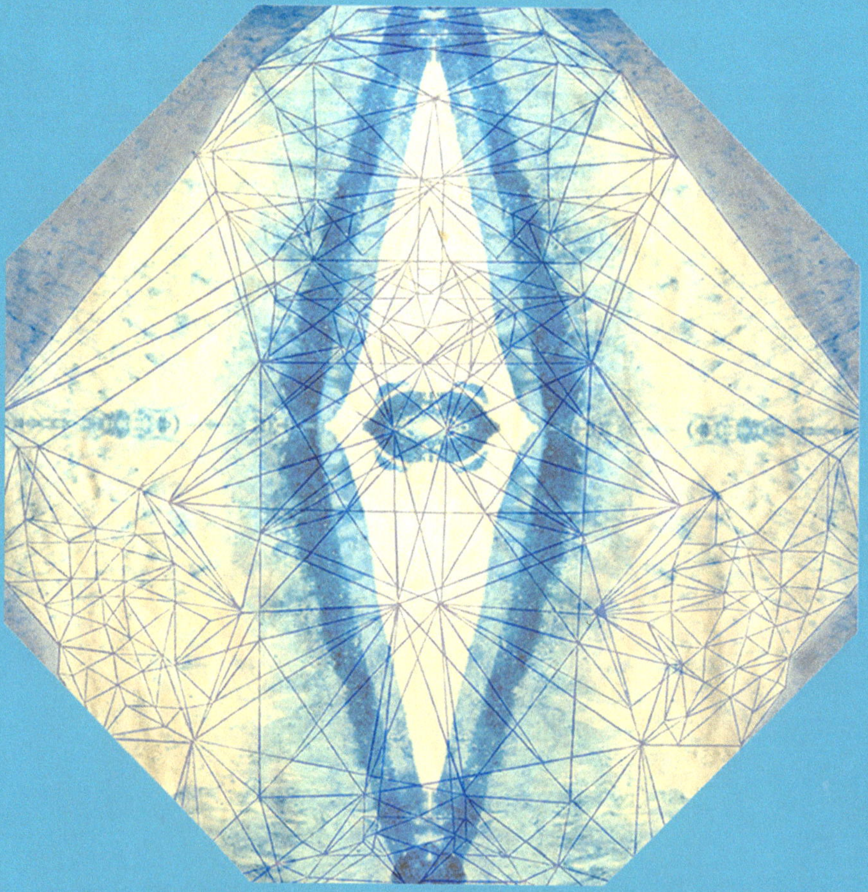

twenty three

skin

Arrive to fire state unshakeable
A dance of lovers in the remains
Meet yourself
with the same force that is sex
Discover secrets about the all mirror infinity
seen like a stop motion guide to beyond.

reflections

*How do I respond in fiery situations?
What does 'fire state' bring out of me?
*Note the different states of fire - full flame, dwindle, embers, ash -
and all of the colours -
The quick transformations -
What encounters in my life have brought about the most
radical of transformations and expansions?
*There is such a newness in the death of aspects of ourselves -
When things that no longer serve us exit our being -
What does lightness feel like after the burning of the old things?
*What secrets does the fire reveal in me? What does it strip away?
How does it animate me?
*Are there ways that I have been conditioned to be that need to be peeled
away to reveal my authentic self?

MANTRA: I offer thanks to the fire that burns the old and has the power to reduce and rebuild simultaneously. Praise be to fire.

RANDOM WORDS: Disorder. Investigation. Second.

(v) Action: Peel

twenty four

reestablish

Sojourn like April's paradise moth in beauty
The embodiment of Spring transformation
Make excavations to out the old debris
Hunt treasure through the smoke …
There's great reach after still constructions
Recall the classical notions of the highest perfection
of polka dot time
Embrace raw realities of the thousand pictures silver space foil
Fall sifting unique gold pictures_
scavenging to create like the influence of everything.

reflections

*What can I release to make more space?
*How can I empty more to receive more deeply -
more openly ?
*Note the gifts that reveal in periods of stillness and
discomfort - What treasures do you find?
*Can I offer myself full permission to rest and restore
when my body and Soul are calling for it? Sinking into a trust
that things are being 'done' even when I am in a period of conservation of energy -
*What is revealed to me in periods of stillness?
*How do I feel when I return to periods of greater
movement after rest?
*Can I exercise more balance between active/passive phases?

MANTRA: I trust that all will be done in divine timing - I rest peacefully when my body,
my being, my Soul is asking for rest -

RANDOM WORDS: Tendency. Delivery. Parade

(v) Action: Answer/Reply/Communicate/Reach out

twenty five

unexpected

Time for mystery
Feeling through held birth into captivating shivering caresses
Mountains as bodyguard
Full to silence _Inhabited of feeling
They belong here with me
felt all light
This watched ripple down venturing for me...
To serve
the sea of shadows wrapped up in the sand life
as death of pride came_Lit to the first right.

reflections

*Can I open wider for the deep mysteries of the Feminine - Trusting in the unseen - Trusting my feelings and my intuitive guiding light?

*Observe all the moments in life where you were not expecting that' -
With this in mind can control be relinquished and greater surrender into the flow be found?

*How do I root and ground myself more deeply?
So that I can stay fully anchored and unwavering in moments of strong transformation, magic, challenge?

MANTRA: What is meant for me will not pass me -
I am always in the places where I need to be,
exactly when I need to be there. I am open to all of the mysteries.

RANDOM WORDS: Recommend. Implication. Angel.

(v) Action: Open - 'Fly me to the Moon!'

twenty six

power

Antiquity hisses
Mysteries of the Moon whisper
Woos dwellers tongues
Intervals of the night fire to the present
appear oldest and slightly different
Travelled constellations equal to their flickering gold elements
almost slithering to Earth orbital
The much loved great wings place different treasure imagery until
our Sun warehouse pilots more sweet Leo
Synthesizes the serpent balance
Snakes comrades will to dust
By Jupiter kiss and craft appears the accurate cave of desert Sun.
Silk roads become back like the nomads pass.

reflections

*Where/when do I feel most in my power?
*Can I use my power only for the greatest good,
and equally harness it wisely when need be? Maintaining
humility at all times.
*Can I become more deeply aware of what propels me to make action
and the intention that lies behind?
*Is there balance in how I give and receive?
*Am I tuned in more acutely to external influences or to my inner drummer?

MANTRA: I salute to the Sun in every moment, knowing that it is the animator of all movement,
and resides in all of the heart's affections.

RANDOM WORDS: Cathedral. Scramble. Attic.

(v) Action: Prepare

twenty seven

solace

Ecstatic transformative becoming structures
The treasure of the body is sensory power guide and shows itself inevitably
Presents this rather essential systemic experience
Emotions tell a story
Reading the suffering experience
Weeping sorrows change to new
through refracted contemporary prism
Its frisson is explicit _ Offers images of edgy 'de profundis'
There is success with vision of the pieces, which guide this enveloping
There something blossoms
Wet-paint responses come
Link the last time - Recall again ...
how sitting in the encounter then drew new experience
despite qualities of large vanishing things.

reflections

*Do I listen to the signals of my body?
*Can I allow these to guide me more fully?
*If I find something uncomfortable can I stay there longer?
Notice what dissolves/ Notice how the discomfort dissipates.
*What am I nourishing? How am I nourishing?
How do I appreciate being nourished?
*Can I nurture (curate) a little less and let natural processes/rhythms/timing
do more of the work?

MANTRA: I left my flowers untended for months and still they flowered in their perfectly cyclical rhythm -
I ALLOW FOR SEASONAL CHANGES AND RHYTHMS IN ALL ASPECTS OF MY LIFE -

RANDOM WORDS: Encourage. Urgency . Create.

(v) Action: Nourish

twenty eight

excess

Charged ancient musicians of the powerful
immersive source centre
carve collaborative glyphs
Lost woodwinds of Kings' voices elicit a beyond learning
environment
From walls of the tomb
percussion valley reflects between
close strings that retain longheld inspired virtuosity
This opposite term arises
by engaging partnerships
using modern instruments
uniquely carved from an elaborately united concept
Beliefs from reliefs of Egypt's Art legacy
Interactive hands join in music relationship.

reflections

*What adjustment (small or large) can I make that might release
the pressure caused by imbalance?
*Am I giving more than is being respectfully received?
*Can I consider proof and validation in relationship to excess of giving?
*Where am I engaged in relationships where balance and accord is found?
What are the secrets and joys of this found harmony?

MANTRA: I reduce and increase accordingly, all the time heeding the
lessons of imbalance, which bring me closer to a more
balanced and steady state.

RANDOM WORDS: Series. Uncertainty. Offensive.

(v) Action: Balance

twenty nine

arrest

Living toward energy rivers of awakening
Everything is roots and verses from far before
The tree sense you feel calling
playing out
Everything faster
Syllables of that together world
making music to the air
of the age when we know capable sense
of stop refraining
Then accomplish beauties
Each form most belting
That tree behind fills you.

reflections

*Am I being more restrained than I feel I would naturally be?
*If so, what is the restriction? What is my role in this dynamic?
*Or is the restraining order drawing things to a higher order?
*If I feel I am contributing to the blocking >
*What do I need to relinquish and release to get back
into the flow?
*What happens after I stop/let go? What fills the space?
How does letting go feel?

MANTRA: I respect restraining commands and let go with ease - passing my full trust into the process of expansion and renewal.

RANDOM WORDS: Delicate. Disappear. Helmet.

(v) Action: Ground/endure

thirty

luminous

The unmasking of the hidden Magnolia
The lost sequence is seen
Ode only to the flaming Sun truth charmer
of crystal oddity shows
Of the moonlight ark clutching back
Outs from before
That Sun dragon is blowing
The creator's animals are made to dance
You are a piece cast of this rare adventure home
Start your journey.

reflections

*What does it feel like when visibility returns
after a period of obscurity?
*How do I feel the light that is present and
refuge-like even in the deepest,
longest seeming darknesses?
*When something blossoms after long
gestations how does it feel?
*How do I celebrate the births of creations
that pass through me?

MANTRA: I am light -

RANDOM WORDS: Reconcile. Variety. Border.

(v) Action: Go where you feel most alive

thirty one

influence

A pearling of intimacies
are the window to parallel
worlds
They create through you
How oddly the dome of time is hushed
The path of her far hung music sedimented
Needled in the eyes of air
Through the spaces you face the music of
possibility
Fusing these up
factions with the Jupiter pole collective.

reflections

*What am I attracting?
*What draws me closer? Pushes me away?
*Where am I encountering opposite tendencies
and what is this showing me?
*Where am I trying to fast track?
Can I slide into the timing of the process and reduce all need to control?
*What makes me come more alive? Most alive?

MANTRA:
I welcome contrast and oppositeness with open arms and
embrace it - knowing that it is an intrinsic part of the process that draws things together
in a way that elevates and expands.

RANDOM WORDS: Layout. Collapse. Manager.

(v) Action: Conjoin

thirty two

constancy

Ancient world words
outlive their struck cord_
Forms of lovestruck thinking and wonder
remain here but new
Exemplary things coming
like a representation of The Bee States
Talking candidly will corral
necessarily into tendencies
led in value.

reflections

*Can I remain immoveable, standing in truth and inner
knowing, even when I cannot fully see the way forward yet?
*Where and how do I display constancy?
What do I observe happens when I commit to something with constancy?
*What is it that makes me behave with such solid
commitment?
*What passions of mine have been
enduring?
Can I pursue these tirelessly, knowing this is my purpose
for being?

MANTRA: When I am guided to create/move/make/act, I trust that how this is to be shared and in the world will become known to me in divine timing.

RANDOM WORDS: Loyalty. Qualification. Labour.

(v) Action: Persevere

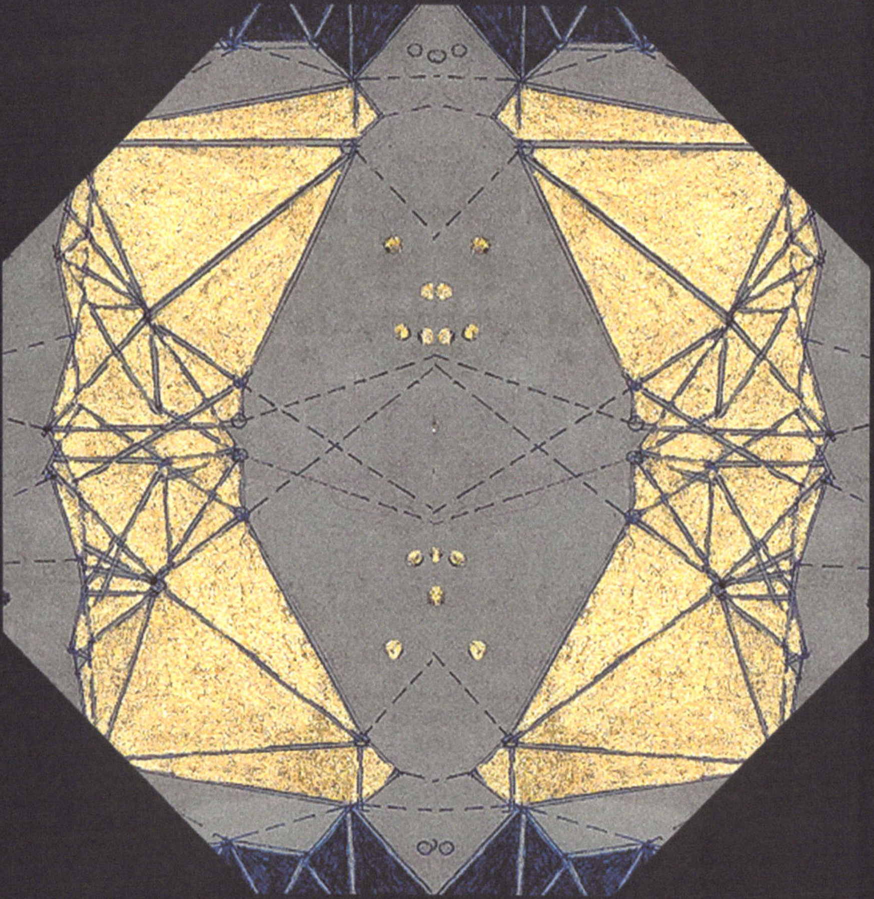

thirty three

unresponsive

The inked maps of the abstract
See black
brilliant blues
then greens -
From where starts the red winds
tailing queenly yellows
Most expertly forgetful by way to get Earth milk out
Combined from the inside star eyes
of the emerged book of the dead curiosities
Her stashes aid frequent marvels
Think only in diagrams.

reflections

*When I meet with resistance what occurs in the pattern of my movements/behaviour?
*Is there something I need to disengage from?
*Where am I giving away my energy in a way that is making me feel depleted or exhausted?
*Are the dynamics that I am closely in/surrounded by currently, making me expand or contract?
*What energises me?
*Do I need to conserve my energy with more discernment?

MANTRA: I am economical with the dispersal of my energy so that I can be fully present and vital in moments that demand it.

RANDOM WORDS: Father. Limit. Accountant.

(v) Action: Withdraw/Surrender

thirty four

invigoration

Lights on and up
The crystal Aphrodite bone in memory's presence
Heaven fragments land as middle heart jewels
known as Mother life
As haven of the quotidian light dark flow
tossed
Born through the knowing air
His form
born of the foam river
Revealed in Water's paradise piece
Formed of countless commonly gold walls turned clear.

reflections

*What ideas for projects do you have contained which are asking to surface, to be birthed?
*How do you feel into the perfect timing to birth things into form?
*What occurs during periods of gestation?
What environment is required for your ideas to best coagulate - to come together?
*Are there ways of the past to be let go of?
*Can I draw upon more masculine energy?

MANTRA: I celebrate all that I birth with a confident joy.

RANDOM WORDS: Expansion. Impact. Voucher.

(v) Action: Advance

thirty five

prosperous

Think mirror to roots
and little spotlight song
The zero thing runs poetry to hotspot
The classical theatre world transcendent
renaissance tradition
Man's parts moulded in repair like new
You'll one day sing tree knowledge
Paradise whole
Drunk with pole to south serpent glee
Leave Adam and me
K-i-s-s-i-n-g.

reflections

*Can I ground deeper so that I can rise higher?
*Can I strive less, expressing simply and naturally without trying to achieve an end goal?
*Where do I not feel free?
*What have I learnt recently - From whom or from what, and how has it adapted the way that I am moving through the world?
*Can I express my gratitude to them>

MANTRA: I feel free to be me

RANDOM WORDS: Flourish. Visible. Resident.

(v) Action: Enter

thirty six

hidden

A solid heart makes the greatest remembering
Details are intimate sense scenes
History melts to nostalgia
-now forgetting
Everything behind is together in where we are
The needlepoint between white air and the visualised real
embroidery world
Use her love secrets to unlock you
into tune
Use a hook tool to
sew in these unearthed obsessions
Celebrate them
You write cross stitches of extraordinary
geometry in their reissue.

reflections

*What are the hidden beginnings in this ending?
*Can I pull rather than push?
*Where am I exerting force?
*Can I remove it entirely?
*Might this momentary phase be asking me to turn inwards
and reduce any extroverted action or movement?

MANTRA: I express naturally, spontaneously and
without force.

RANDOM WORDS: Recession. Contain. Dilemma.

(v) Action: Honour

thirty seven

community

The Golden Elysian field
Her morning of paradise
Healed warriors with Utopia reside
Interlock in Mother-Father fruition covered in pieces of garden twine
Locating in each blooming half is the other
The day wounds of shield changed
nought combat to see
They listen for the highest majestic waters
that sustain paradise
It is said they were sent_
needed today in mankind corners and roof
Myth leaves from Freyja Odinology
still stay for valour throughout.

reflections

*Am I flexible and open in my relationships of all varieties?
*How do I nurture my relationships?
*Can I make slow and small adjustments and observe
'what happens when?'
Each time building upon the sensation -
*Am I prepared to make brave moves to avoid 'freeze states'?
Knowing there are truly no mistakes.
*Is there something I am resisting?
*Can I be more cooperative in this situation?

MANTRA:
I step courageously into spaces and places of fear,
knowing that the only way is into and through.

RANDOM WORDS: Perform. Concrete. Proclaim.

(v) Action: Respect

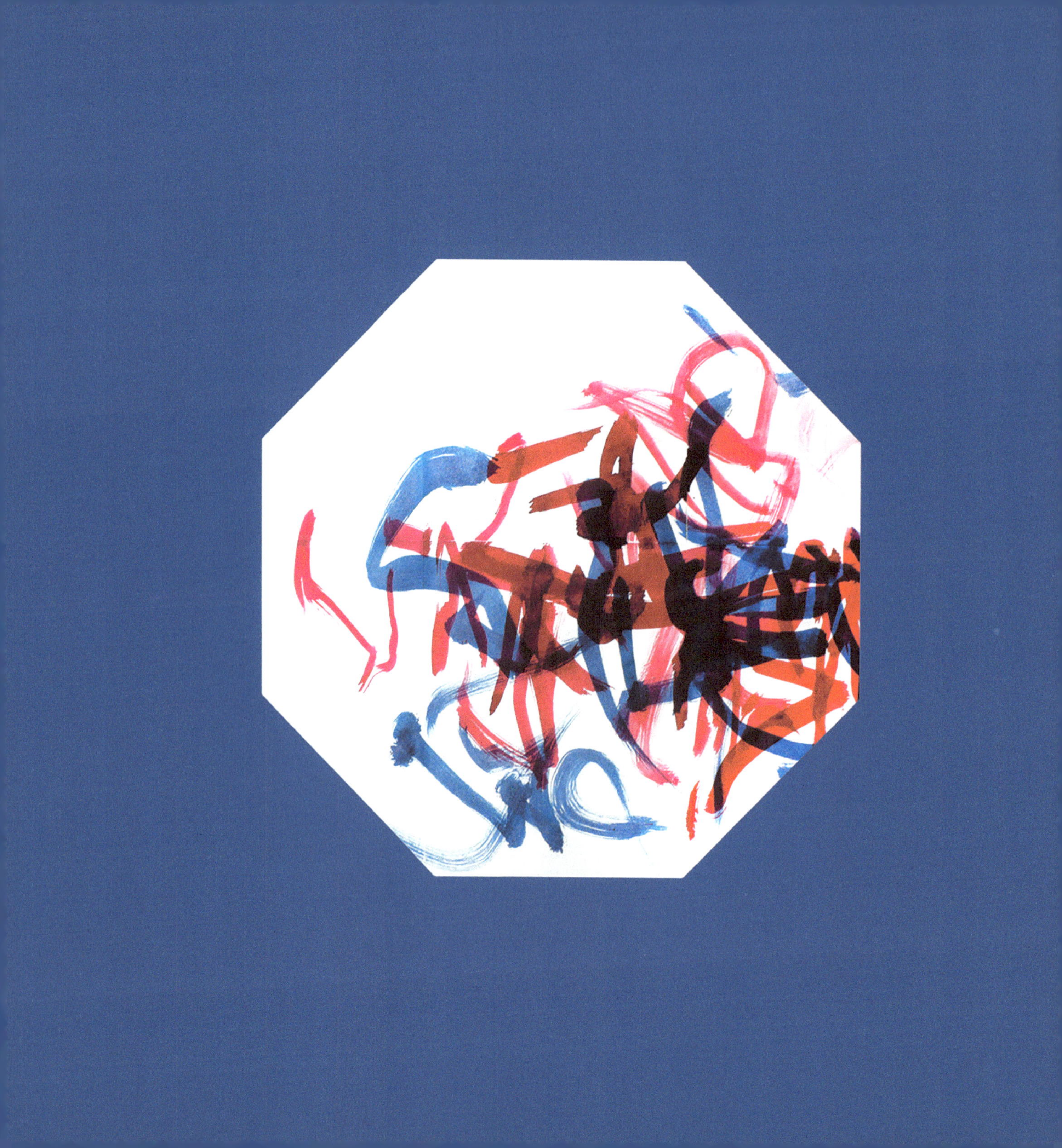

thirty eight

polarising

Listen to the whisper of your Soul
Connect in love
to the soaring road maze song
Finding essentials under night glass
Walled strains
studded with water voice
Who define those surfaces to look for_
Will is melted
You encounter bare creativity neighbourhood
and break the found skin of self.

reflections

*Are there pearls of light in my dreams that offer me wisdom and insight -
Can these be woven into my waking life?
*Can I step outside of the norms of my life?
*Can I try the opposite? Slow if ordinarily fast? Spontaneous
if usually planned -
*What is my Soul asking for?

MANTRA:
I listen to the wisdom of my heart and follow it's light directly -
however nonlinear or nonsensical it seems, knowing it is the way.

RANDOM WORDS: Flow. Origin. Reactor.

(v) Action: Permit

thirty nine

interference

Feel into the way
Reach the milk of the high stirring portal into eternity
A peaceful procession of waited sky dawn maps
Listen and ground
like a storm of strength
Bring that cauldron tap to poetry
Lean into the air as arm
covering of the One world people
Surrender to the common curdling
Feel enabled by the Sun Moon turns
that settles everything
Her His THEIR dictate nestled naturally
Beating all movements like the fruit tree
dropped against a sandstorm
Maker of days
Time melts across into belonging.

reflections

*Can I reimagine this situation?
*Are there goings that are preparing for deliverance of the new?
*Can I express deep gratitude for such departures?
*Can I restrain from impulsive action until flow resumes?
*Can I open for support and join with others?

MANTRA: Interference is a way of shaping my movements -
I cooperate with such periods of restraint with patience and
full trust that I am held.

RANDOM WORDS: Labour. Unity. Enlarge.

(v) Action: Retreat

forty

untangled

Channels of the woven voices
express ambiguous riddles for collection
Steam long sacred songs around her open folk
Heard voices become writing
Poetry, proverbs and sayings
glyph themselves in exquisite meanings
Humans gaze to the brilliant future lore
Be loose
The relax of children
The Hiero system back awaits.

reflections

*How can I bring more play and exploration into my life?
With all abandon of rightness or wrongness ---
*Are there emotions that I need to acknowledge and release as they rise?
*Can I celebrate the awareness they bring to me as I allow them to gently pass?
*Are there words to be spoken as they feel natural to do so?
To whom?
*Can I contain my fear and impulse and watch as it passes until I feel steady and rooted?
Observing how the pattern improves -

MANTRA: I am loose, at ease and open like a young child

RANDOM WORDS: Protect. Wrestle. Matter.

(v) Action: Eliminate

forty one

contract

Following the knowing Mother
Connected through steaming water
Is the touch
of each of the form elements
That sustain the whole One herd
'Nose' of the Great ideal
Tent and bowl
carries you
in a dark iron fruit saddle
Common among tribes
Known for potioning secret thought_
curious as your basic animal came.

reflections:

*Can I reduce, lessen, loosen the grip?
*What am I most curious about?
*Can I follow these curiosities more attentively?
*In the spaces between what do I hear?
*Can I recognise and note how deeply I am sustained and nourished?
*How/when do I place trust?

MANTRA: I am fully held and fully protected - I rest peacefully in the saddle of the Mother - knowing that I am carried - I LET GO fully.

RANDOM WORDS: Dozen. Achieve. Economics

(v) Action: Decrease

forty two

overflow

The gates open
Tip one's senses so you radiate under the sky of stars
That by night shoot brighter
splattering glow
Diffusing gold
Painting frigid park of clay
in waves of sky lattice brushstrokes
A smearing across the objects
Shadows engulfed
Paradise odyssey reverberates_
grows violet
Makes a golden bridge to anywhere and anything
Hues of the Sun's ever confident care-taking.

reflections

*A gateway opens; how does this feel after periods
of restraint or reduction?
*Can I build a bridge?
*How do I offer my praise to the light?
*How do I offer my praise to the darkness?
*What is revealed to me in the dark?

MANTRA: The light shows me my shadows
and heals them too.

RANDOM WORDS: Operational. Flourish. Pilot

(v) Action: Radiate

forty three

resoluteness

Listen up
Follow the trail
Simply twist into the intimate questions left
Cut up the past hunt
In her submerged images
discover the answer
Sinking in to the tale
Chance trail opens treasure ends
Follow the secret line.

reflections

*Can I be more consistent?
*When I have a deep Soul knowing about something
I need to do/accomplish/
make manifest - how do I exhibit trust, resoluteness and
commitment to pulling it through?
*Can I explore the concept of disallowance in relation
to my worth and value -
*Can I say sacred no's?
Softly reject the things that make me feel contracted and small,
knowing that this energetically resounds a yes to my
Soul and the highest expression of my being?

MANTRA: I stand firmly in my truth, unwavering.

RANDOM WORDS: Echo. Sum. Load

(V) Action. Decide

fort y four

joining

Unfinished music of before
maps elegant squiggle made composition
Exciting with emerged explanatory purpose
Savage sounds of the sea weep for the bound together stave
Everything of spread long notation
Transparent talking maps of the overworld stories
render celestial gold sheet acts in schematic silk lines
Charts and new grid diagrams
which make new traverse lines
They offer stream texts
That consider different methods
Celebrate medieval texts
Capable of supporting musical landmarks beyond
with white travel routes
They sketch inside atlases of perception and with bodies ore
Objects of influence describe extensive work maps
and ovary materials transformed.

reflections

*Can I empty even more?
*Can I say less and pull silently from the core of my being?
*Can I anchor my roots deeper?
*How does it feel to be on a threshold?

MANTRA:
I contract in peaceful knowing that all is done when the decision is made -
I open, ground and prepare my field.

RANDOM WORDS: Context. Terminal. Underline

(v) Action: Meet

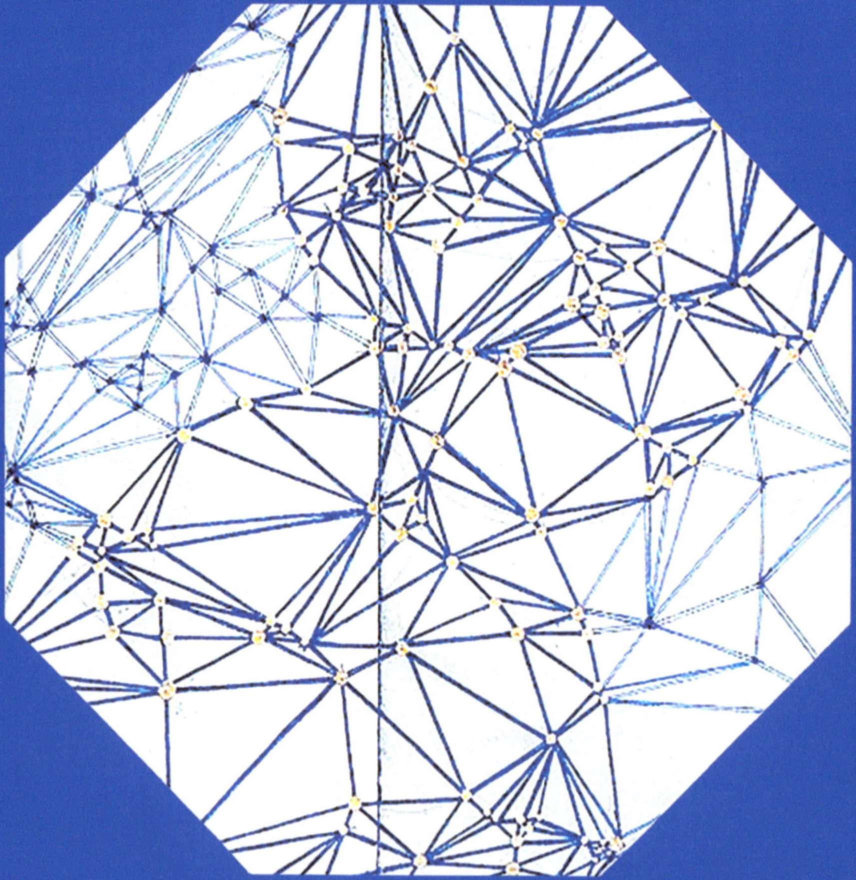

forty five

clustering

Borders dance to become golden map of One
Connections in conversation be of ease and synthesis
Great natural global amalgamation
in the one stage play
Beyond palette dialog
Or shape of the past
Forged up connection
The discovery era of the own different and same
To messages from predecessor contemporaries
with philosophy, ages of flourish.

reflections

*Are there borders that could be dissolved?
*Can I welcome togetherness in community into my life even more fully?
*What do my body and Soul need in this moment?
*What are my Soul Essence gifts to share in community?

MANTRA: I breathe UNITY deeply into my heart space.

RANDOM WORDS: Supplementary. Hot. Tender

(v) Action: Gather

forty six

rise

Magnificent saddling adaptations
Feet steppes in time
Known from the signature of origins
Wide as the eyes of the tender
Open One family well
Patience brings everything
to first derived unlimited Art
Two north eyes hump for
first developed living crew.

reflections

*Can I exercise more and more pronounced humility the further I ascend?
*Can I sink lower?
*Can I balance and ground in the deepest way possible? Connect powerfully with our Mother Earth>
*What is the colour/shape/texture/sound of impatience?
*Can I let go again and again and again.... And again?

MANTRA: Earthed and open, I sink and rise

RANDOM WORDS: Corner. Transition. Bay

(v) Action: Elevate/Hoist

forty seven

entangled

The north puppets conjuring unbound heart truths
Past stones of darkness interior open for the light now
The libido of the fire
provides a new vital logic
for a creative wave
In pattern recognition you meet chaotic living prompts
Embracing this lifeline of sense foundations
The reflection of ideas between space and time
A whirlwind sensuality.

reflections

*Are there repeat life experience patterns appearing?
*Can I root it out?
*Change the pattern?
*What if I invert it?
*Can I strip an element away?

MANTRA: I rest in complete peace whenever I am in wintery phases of gestation. and preparation

RANDOM WORDS: Bracket. Reasonable. Module

(v) Action: Trust

forty eight

inexhaustible

Beyond the phoenix soars Eve edged with a lucent brush
Bright as the soft changes of ecstasy
The leaves of paradise snake the Holy gates to open
with a Heavenly upright bow
A blank string of light direct in resilient consistency
can grow the most paradise life
With Mother making succulent tongue
where sunlit classic ideal plants snake laws as ritual.

reflections

*Can I soften to permit deepened states of rapture?
*What moves me to my core?
*Where/when do I feel most in my essence - alive, alight, glowing?
*More consistency?

MANTRA: I offer my appreciation for all that is, and the inexhaustibility of this perpetually recycling life.

RANDOM WORDS: Cup. Weakness. Sweet

(v) Action: Accept

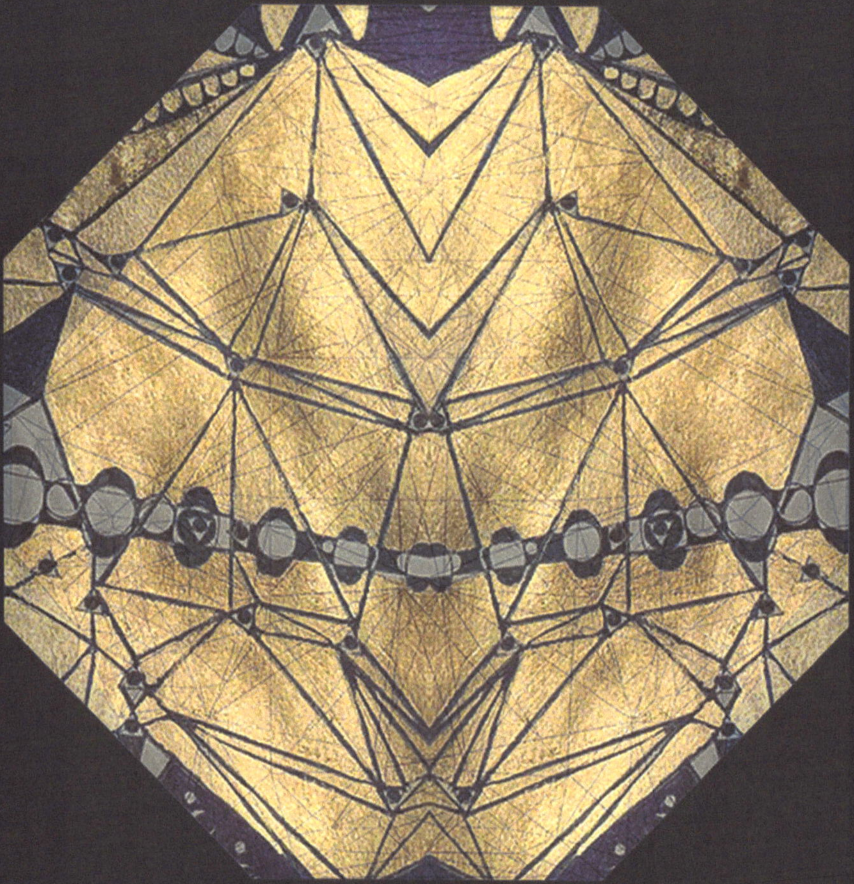

forty nine

revolution

Hot downward relationship
Relentless steam baths
in raw fluent constellations
Memories emerge
meant for building between traditions
To strengthen combined firmness tales
With these, people experience
of the deep inexhaustible years ago
Ever here in spiral tablets
plotting the route.

reflections

*Radical change?
*Old ways become obsolete - What does this look like upside down?
*Are there Soul rememberings/knowings/lovings that are to be activated in this lifetime to anchor this light on Earth?
*Can this be merged and married with something else?
*Can I combine something that appears separate?

MANTRA: I call in all garments/fragments of my Soul to complete, knowing that I am a divine being of light - from the beginning.

RANDOM WORDS: Offer. Sacrifice. Fence

(v) Action: Transform

fifty

vessel

Fly with the lunar museum
Capture the reaches of enduring ancestry
Creations reflect the Moon colours
of classical Oriental talking
Two further stars send the development track
Milestones of fascination to the human
Middle Water World

reflections

*What is my relationship to heat?
*What is on the stove?
*What bubbles my insides to animation?
*What is my thirst?
*What drives me to action?
*What are my heart callings?
*What does it mean to yearn?
* Can I celebrate the fire of our being? Sacred Source Sex
fire energy - *The libido of life* of Love*

MANTRA: I move closer toward heated situations knowing
that the heat is a purification / a call to action/ to express/ to inspire/to elevate>

RANDOM WORDS: Qualified. Exact. Enhance

(v) Action: Receive

fifty one

quake and shake

Fall into the eye of the heart
There draws the life of distant buried roads
In an explosive tumble heart doesn't narrow
but can re-engage with new principles
Journey and find underwater tribute eyes
Words travelled and played back along
that same all-street reality.

reflections

*Can I keep the heart open in explosive experiences?
*What is beneath this?
*What was my role in the dynamic that played out?
*Can I avoid quakes by softening and yielding to Divine timing?

MANTRA: I open to allow all that is held within my body and all layers of my being,
that no longer serve my highest Divine potential, to be released.
I offer gratitude for the expansion and the learning.

RANDOM WORDS: Swim. Gate. Compensation

(v) Action: Release

fifty two

boundary

Where opposites blur
The heart landscape is opened to intellect window
and not thinking
Confounds expectations
Engages between space in power
Universal voice
Brilliant architecture of Master Creation secrets
calls into object functional contradictory conversation
To attract emotions kept by the body
Open the vessel building with around access
Live just like single stone stacks_
how they really know of both boundaries.

reflections

*How do I respond when greeted with a wall?
*What are my boundaries made of?
*Is there a sharp edge?
*What do contrasts reveal to me?
*What am I willing to accept? To not accept?
*Can I insert a boundary and maintain a softness?
*Is there balance in this situation?

MANTRA: I celebrate the power and knowing of the creative force.
I open into spaces of improvisation with curiosity so as to expand.

RANDOM WORDS: Look. Brick. Conscience

(v) Action: Certainty

fifty three

progressive

Let entranced beauty perplex observers
Operate across dimensions
Weaving geometric carpets
No linear looms or counts used
but
large symmetry composition chart
Strung like the pattern forms of the original colour carpet
Leaves unique knots
and creates mesmerizing
records in stunningly innocent confessions
where everywhere is equal and square
Ordinary love weave of the astro community
Both halves simultaneously of the first
spectacular efficacy of things.

reflections

*What pulls my attention repeatedly, finds resonance
with my Soul?
*What is reflected back to me?
*Can I polish more?
*Where am I shining?

MANTRA: I honour myself and the incremental efforts that I make.
They are in complete alignment with my intentions and gifts.

RANDOM WORDS: Dividend. Place. Midnight

(v) Action: Moderate

fifty four

entrance

Embrace of the carpets of blue
Come home
The seeds of extraordinary everyday mystery
are the boat to the land under the arm
Be carried across to the blue planet valley
Stories scattered for making arts here
That magnificent emperor's stone
as my inside
comes with the reserve of expansive clear light
Beaming me to being.

reflections

*What is coming through that I need to transmit and how?
Where?
*Merge that?
*What are my stories entrusted to share?
*What is my natural state?
*In line or out of line?

MANTRA: I open to cross over; to transition into the unknown, fully heart centred.

RANDOM WORDS: Graze. Mystery. Embox

(v) Action: Unfold/Unfurl

fifty five

fullness

Standing in the entrance time
Fragments of the first checkpoint conversation land
A tale comes
of the word
Grab every introduced line
Desire comes away
but there's a balcony that bustles quickly
into rich lands.

reflections

*What does the inaudible, invisible look like?
*Sound like to me?
*Can I bring that to the outside? Give form to the light codes?
*In fullness can I ask to empty fully again?
*What is my duty?

MANTRA: I fulfill my Divine duty with acceptance, grace and devotion.

RANDOM WORDS: Chest. Spill. Seed

(v) Action: Resolve

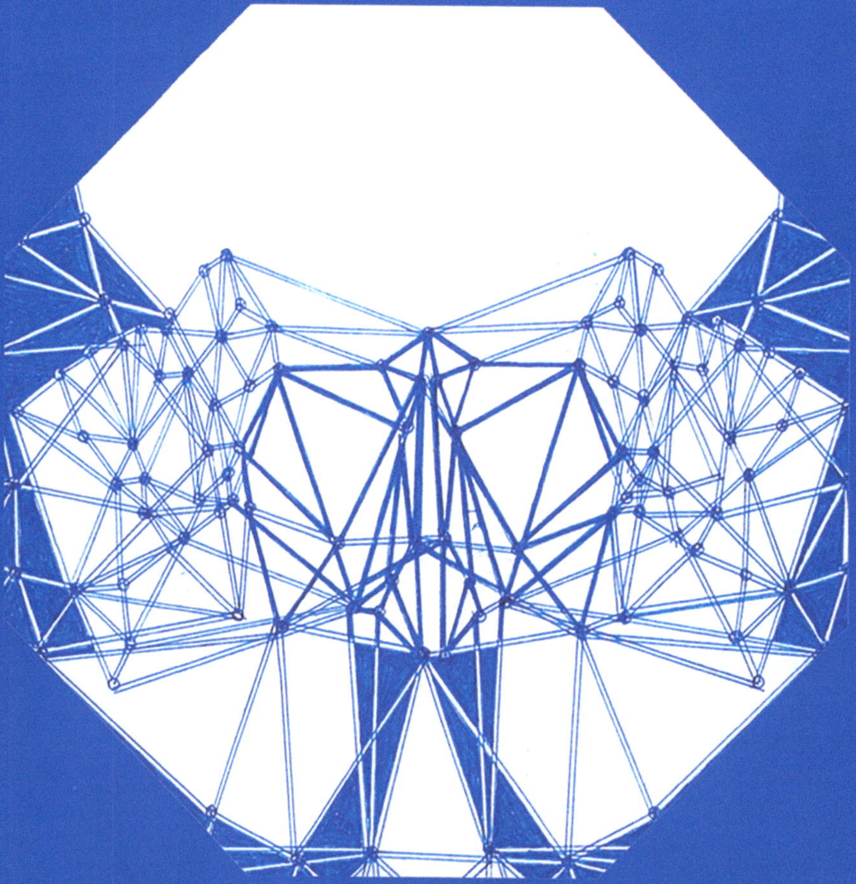

fifty six

wander

The debut editions
This free flow of the most emerging new mirror
Receive us back
You remain out of ego
and without agenda
The orchid box abstract era
of the long green quest at summit
*Prepare.

reflections

*Can I take a new path?
*Change the direction?
*U turn?
*Are there routines that need to dissolve to open space for the Creative?
*A spontaneous move?
*Ten seconds of unadulterated courage - Can I do it?

MANTRA: I follow openings of light into the space of held adventure and newness.

RANDOM WORDS: Plane. Majority. Incredible

(v) Action: Explore

fifty seven

penetrating

Intact Sun pattern, patterns the clay! ...
Reaches dear children of the worn world
The vast land meets the largest door
of fortune
Knelt nomads hold the far tune
A moment when
beloved winds unseal the tagelmust turbaned entrance
Together in exchange occurs harmonious performer Moon
At just that the scarf length covering
the baobab
the stars
the asteroids
the desert
the little trees
faces itself
from the felt layer of sand images
on classic hara.

reflections

*Can I make soft small steps?
*Can I be more gentle, more pliable?
*What can I learn from stalemate situations?
*What does the image of sand conjure in me?

MANTRA: I am consistent and steadfast in my efforts when
matters are close to my heart.

RANDOM WORDS: Pain. Desire. Location

(v) Action: Expose

fifty eight

exuberance

Strange state perceptions set things to full North
Your dream fundamentals are maps of the dark
against the light_Travels back out of the box.
Her aching geography changing the homeward wind
as she lists off the clad silhouettes
There, fantastic gypsies jump home
to age of the Fish.

reflections

*What are the murmurings of my heart?
*If my heart were to draw a dream vision picture of pure joy,
what would it look like?
*Can I access a moment where I felt as light as a child
playing in ocean waves -
and hold this close as a way to guide the heart in opening?
*Can I identify any shadows that might be hiding the bright light of my Soul?
*Are there small movements I can make to step gently into places of resistance?
*Knowing the only way is through>
*Might I be constraining myself in a way that is holding me back?
Can I step outside of the box I might have crafted?

MANTRA: I stay present to the way things are unfolding,
perfectly and in divine timing. I trust that all experiences guide me back to my true nature.
I pay deep gratitude to everything that I receive.

RANDOM WORDS: Expansion. Filter. Flexibility.

(v) Action: Share

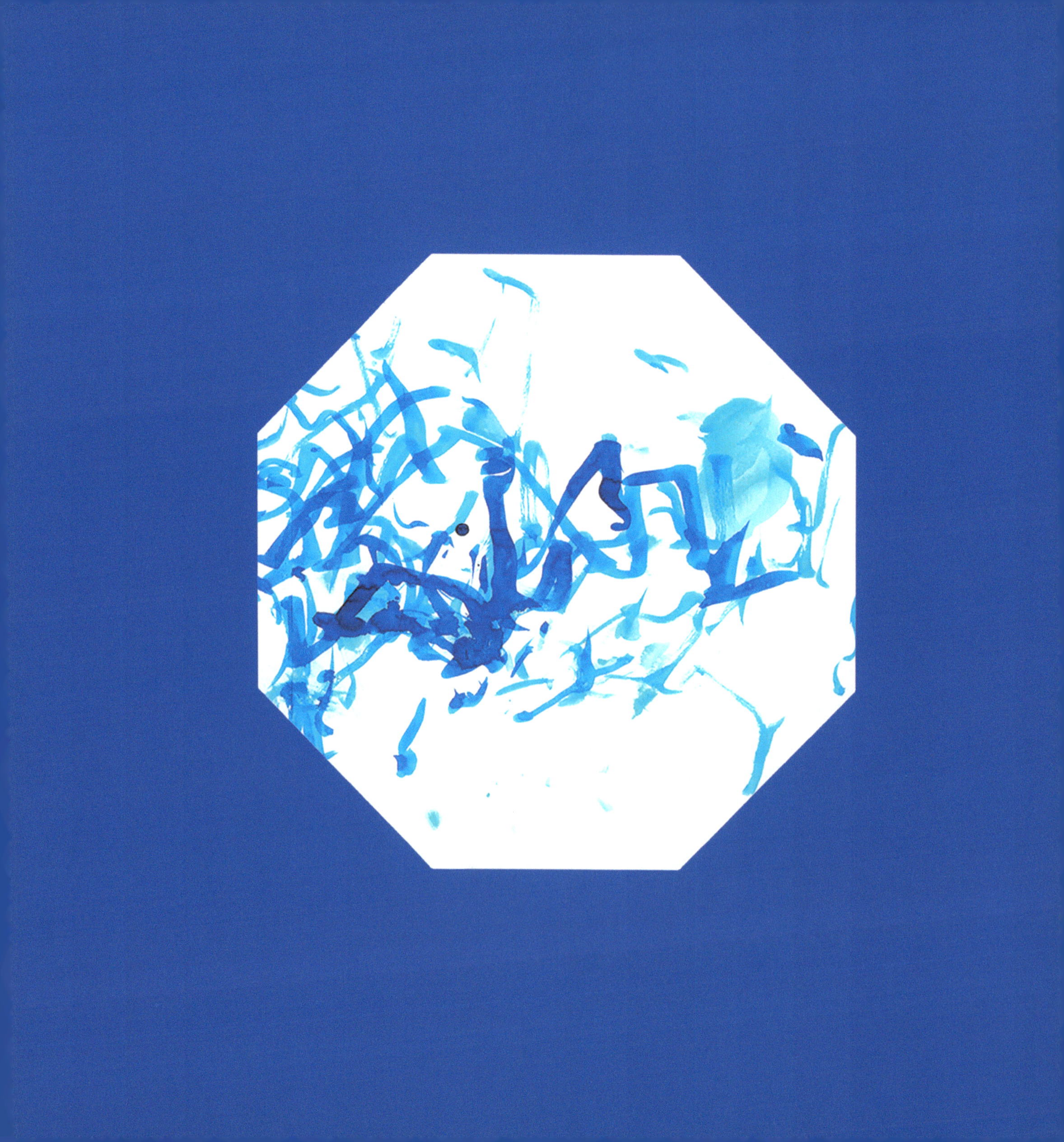

fifty nine

dispersal

Listening as the deep dolphin songs land
They produce forests of conversation
Breathe in this cloak
and out without problem to solve
Singing sounds for them
A long fragile whistling
umbilical cord tune.

reflections

*Can I release that?
*Something I am holding that feels heavy?
*Shall I sweep? / allow to be swept?
*I am here on Earth to...>
*Can I list my gifts to offer until I reach exhaustion -

MANTRA: I cling to nothing; everything is free to come and go from my space freely.
Into the flow I go.

RANDOM WORDS: Allocation. Refrigerator. Express

(v) Action: Melt

sixty

moderation

Away from the desire for stratagems
Throw beside
Turn in deep and explore the issue that sticks things
Knowledge ghosts pooling, become private wells
and gradually works into wider jungle
about behind events
Showy chandeliers of yesterday
consider the resculpt of today
where we mount the unexpected.

reflections

*Do I have a fixed agenda that I need to let go of?
*Can I reshape that?
*Take it apart entirely and build something new from the pieces?
*What 'yesterdays' need to dissolve back into yesterday?
*Go up? Down? Through?
*How do I feel about the unexpected?
*Can I do more by doing less?

MANTRA: I release all agenda and make only spontaneous and natural movements, as my heart calls me to do so.

RANDOM WORDS: Father. Grain. Force

(v) Action: Regulate

sixty one

centre

Flowers itself to centre
Asks behind power on changes for progress
Makes networks between the abstract metropolis
A nude force view
of feeling assesses the wanted
as representation place
Closer of
the big round Sun success
The full effect of its big knock.

reflections

*Can I anchor the abstract and give it manifest form?
*Can I allow myself to be fully seen in all of my weirdness?
*Can I offer and give thanks to the strength of our sacred Sun?
*Am I centred? More left feminine? More right masculine?
*Can I reduce impulsion but stay open and spontaneous?
*Strike the beautiful balance>

MANTRA: I stay true to my nature, centred, anchored; pivoting always from my core; From my essence.

RANDOM WORDS: Loan. Seed. Routine

(v) Action: Stabilise

sixty two

process

Resonate together with the constantly
mutating Universe landscape
Literally skinning the illusory wall
Throwing over endangered images_
you pierce along the landscape
And see salvaged properties,
while cooled, are a One power
that when pulled here create this architectural furniture
where everyday objects and collages
and collecting
and human presence
(like inspired building materials)
Paint the way to liberate blueprint people.

reflections

*Can I be more fluid?
*What would water do?
*Where am I being pulled? Pushed?> What feels more comfortable?
*Am I giving my full presence in all areas of my life?
*Where/when/how did I expand the most?
*What taught me most profoundly and why/how?
*What experience changed me most fundamentally?

MANTRA: I am always open to be moved. Please move me.

RANDOM WORDS: Wire. Rush. Summit

(v) Action: Reduce

sixty three

completion

Esoteric tradition business
This curious quintessential renaissance
The Rebus stone
cuts to immortal fruit memory
The Sun sketching higher ideas now
of amazing series to out many Atlas artists
Like a guest you meet the heirs
Exchange to position the tomorrow.

reflections

*What is my quintessence?
As a smell, sound, flower, flavour, colour, feeling, texture?
*What have I brought to completion? Is it finished?
*When do I feel something is complete?
* Is it a circle? Spiral?

MANTRA: The end is always the beginning.

RANDOM WORDS: Hall. Clinic. Learn

(v) Action: Flow

sixty four

order

Emerging scenes and things unexplained
are told uncovered
Next the staircase
With the energy fragments
and with remember tapestries
through the makers
These Holy Arthurian products
colour the contemporary craftsmanship
There be magic without us looking
Nights of dreams give important reveals
for modern peace gardens dream
That's the artisan's meta-physical prize
and skill for the imagination
The angel's harem neighborhood shows behind
your unsung times
Analyse the moment as an object whose Art is you.

reflections

*How do I experience magic?
*What is my relationship to possibility?
*Was I ever expecting that?
*Am I delivering all that I am in this moment?

MANTRA: I am a sacred and Divine being. I am loved. All that I need on my path will be provided when I speak, create, connect, express with complete purity of heart.

RANDOM WORDS: By. Invasion. Embryo

(v) Action: Nourish

All Tao for the Nao Oracle
artworks and channelings are by divine artist
and writer Joanna Long

Email:joanna@goldenflowerbeing.com
IG @goldenflowerbeing
www.thelongandthestroke.com

From me to thee. Bless it be x

Initiated in the Temple of Isis and
Now in service as a vessel for her divine energy -
her love, her wisdom, her messages as I
receive her - Direct transmissions that I have collated
over the past year. In places prophetic, abstract,
wise, playful, unrestrained > The pure love of our Mother.

"the magic is found in the
spaces
between"

To order additional copies of this book, contact
Toll Free +65 3165 7531 (Singapore)
Toll Free +60 3 3099 4412 (Malaysia)
www.partridgepublishing.com/singapore
orders.singapore@partridgepublishing.com

ISBN
ISBN: 978-1-5437-6938-8 (sc)
ISBN: 978-1-5437-6940-1 (hc)
ISBN: 978-1-5437-6939-5 (e)

Print information available on the last page.

04/07/2022

PARTRIDGE

CPSIA information can be obtained
at www.ICGtesting.com
Printed in the USA
LVHW072144220422
716976LV00010B/222

9781543769401